FROM HERE ON

Four Sunday Drives

Don Thompson

FUTURECYCLE PRESS
www.futurecycle.org

Copyright © 2017 Don Thompson
All Rights Reserved

Published by FutureCycle Press
Athens, Georgia, USA

ISBN 978-1-942371-42-7

He can't reach the inside of anything from the outside... [but] needs to penetrate first into the inner life of a thing, by a moral participation; and then perhaps the outer form may acquire a meaning for him.

—Santayana in *The Last Puritan*

Contents

Granite Road | 7
White Wolf Grade | 15
Corn Camp Road | 23
Quaking Aspen | 30

A Note on the Latin | 39
Acknowledgments | 41

Granite Road

On Granite Road: Crows
dawdle along narrow, crumbling shoulders,
by choice earthbound
and not compelled, not held down like us.
Stubbornly undisturbed,
they take flight only if forced.

The sky's an easy out
these crows wisely refuse,
choosing to bear witness to us
who are half-crazed and grounded
(except in rare dreams)
until earth molders flesh and bone.

But then...

Faced for now with terminus,
that translucid shadow
cast by the ghost we call self,
let crows offer comfort:
Receive it: See

how they strut with notorious panache,
though footsore, vain
but not easily flattered;
how they feast
on leftovers the Lord provides,
panem nostrum quotidianum,
content with whatever they get
their beaks into...

Let watching them be balm:

Let peace come.

Death's not the end,
merely another nondescript dry creek

like this one—Poso,
where the road descending
makes a hard left onto the bridge
that crosses a two-bit Styx.

Easily said...

But downstream, where the creekbed
vanishes into sand and brambles
leaving no trace,
a girl's discarded bones:
Dental records recognized Yoselin's smile.

So pray for grace, for snow falling
on Greenhorn Summit
and falling again all winter,
heaped up until spring
deeper than dry summer doubt.

Pray that run-off would reach up
and touch the bridge,
just touch,
washing its brushwood debris
down into the Valley,
settling there in shallow pools,
quiet pools someone could sit by
and remember Yoselin...

Selah...

On the creek's far side, vandals
who've whacked chunks from history,
who've pry-barred a plaque from its concrete block
(commemorating—what?)
have done no harm to time.
None.
But the old brass
they sold for a dime bag.

We used to abandon brass,
considered worthless,
at that low but abrupt bluff nearby
(fenced now and the fence disrespected)
where dads when we had them
taught us to plink:

no sound more elemental,
more gratifying
to inclinations in a boy's heart
than that unmistakable, metallic clunk
of a bolt chambering a round,
even a .22 short;

no, nothing unless it's steel
honed on oiled whetstone—
somehow combining swish with sizzle,
both silk and grit.

Evidence of wicked delight we take
in breaking things,
this bloodbath of shattered glass
glittering in dirt
like sunlight on water,
impossibly beautiful:

an ossuary for bottles.

Here and there from an intricate pipe
schemata you might doodle,
bored in church,
steam rises reminding us
of how quickly our fierce, insistent breath
whiffs into nothingness.

Our breath, we believe, and our prayers
ascend like the smoke of incense;
they do,
but also mingle with oilfield effluvia.

The earth's poisoned here, sparse
dead weeds like patches of fur
on a rotted carcass.
Hundreds of pumpjacks bend the knee,
knock foreheads on the ground
continuously—worshipers
of a despised but indispensable god
whose minds never wander.

And here this morning, again,
this addled old man sees his breath,
no less awestruck than a toddler;
witnesses its dissipation
with a shrug, without regrets.

Easily said...

Now in Advent, spring's prophesy,
grass like thin, green mist
that burns to dun by afternoon,
blurs the hills.
These flatland slabs upended eons ago
have aged well, venerable,
their rough edges abraded—
deep, angular arroyos
weathered to mere wrinkles.

And everywhere granite nudges consciousness.

No one can ignore volcanic scat
with mica glinting in it like rime:
modest but odd outcrops
and anonymous tors salient enough
to earn local names—
yet nameless,
though marred by graffiti.

Granite, unlike marble,
is much too fractious to chisel,

even for gravestones, and resists
with lithe-chthonic obstinance
any shape we'd want to give it.

So let vandals spray paint:
let them spit.
Their own names
will fade to ghostliness before they die.

And all the stand-alone boulders
will sit on their thumbs,
mum, keeping every secret
ever trusted to them
until commanded to speak—
when and if none of us
remember to offer praise.

The burned saloon's floor is thin air.
At Granite Station
you can stop and listen to the dead
who seem to come here for a drink,
scraping muddy, manured boots—
a sound like wind inhibited by frigid weeds.

They must hang their hats
on nails hammered into oblivion;
lean against the bar,
waxed in old photos to catch the light
that's still here;
then cough up dust clots and look around
for a brass cuspidor
(stolen and sold).

An odd haunting:

Reticent, with sidelong glances,
they watch, expecting
us to manifest next to them...
Will we nod at each other
in the dark mirror?

Instead of brimstone, stale beer
fouls their Sheol,
and ashes, maybe, but no flames:

Only the chimney endures
in this world, stubbornly
making its claim against time.
No smoke, but wisps of fog
in loco fumus
diffuse above it this morning.
The scorched hearth is cold.

Also cold, this other chimney
of rough fieldstone, unfinished
like the past that
keeps shifting its own paradigms,
will easily outlast
the ramshackle cabin attached to it.

Someone must have cashed out here,
done in by drought or a weak beef market,
by alcohol or an unfaithful wife's
escape to town.

Whitewash has washed to gray,
sun-blistered on walls out of plumb;
glass shattered (of course)
and the corrugated roof bloodstained by rust,
one sheet peeled back
as if the wind has been picking scabs...

The dead die without us: Ennui
kills them again and again.
Unless we allow them to haunt,
they fade—disintegrate,
survived by tattered curtains
in windows where they waited for so long,
hoping we'd come.

The solitude here hurts.

But a Hereford bull loitering alone
looks used to it—bleary,
an old fool years from his last mad rut,
ignoring the cows that ignore him,
muttering into the grass.

Cut loose from lust, unfettered,
and no longer troubled by
bells in the dark,
the bull broods over his salt lick,
worries it to a nub:
slow work, glum contentment.

No feedlot at least—
no fear:
rather than a nail gun between the eyes,
a slow, slobbery unraveling.

Offer this prayer then:
to shuffle into eternity
disheveled and stiff-jointed,
grating on everyone's nerves,
and then wake
weightless and well-lubed.

New...

And let the backhoe gouge a hole
for unnecessary bones.
We'll do well
to lie down among the locals
not far from Marah, the town
where no one drinks the water
but only beer—less bitter.

The season's bleak, clouds defeated;
evergreens grieve, almost black.
The grass here died standing tall.

Leaves blown against a gravestone
hide the name:
at least Beloved is legible.

No one blames the wind
or calls the bare trees crass
for letting go. They had to.

But let's sweep the leaves away,
gently, as if brushing hair
from a sleeping child's cheek,

and read again the name,
so ordinary, that endures
only because the chisel insists.

It's raining now, almost: a mist.
And the narrow, burnt-charcoal asphalt—
wicked switchbacks steeply uphill
from here on—begins to glisten.

Everything does...

Somehow this light's not reflected
but seeps out of the earth,
drips from granite:
an immanence:
Scrub oaks exude a sacred sheen
as peace
rises from root to branch.

Dona nos pacem.

And even if the road holds up
its rusted, gut-shot sign to daunt us
—Slippery When Wet—
so what?
Cautiously, we climb.

White Wolf Grade

Color has come and gone once more
on these gnarled, senescent almonds,
down to their farewell crop
this year (maybe)
and overdue for uprooting.
Then tentative saplings,
each with its own stake to cling to,
will take their place, their soil—
will assume their unnamed appellation.

Penitent, they've renounced
blossoms for Lent:
some not quite pink, some white
with an indiscernible celadon glaze,
petals simulate diffuse snow
fallen last night on Bear Mountain—
melted by afternoon
and these faux flakes blown away.

Their buds too minuscule to see from the road,
the trees appear to be as bare
this month as in December, skeletal,
though not bleached by frost.
But we know without doubt
that spring has them in hand,
finally.

Exultate Deo!

Bees splat against the windshield,
only a few but each loss felt:
a faint crack
like hearing the Eucharist fractioned
from a back pew.
Their migrants' hovels, looking abandoned
beside the grove, must teem
with life, with untamed honey lust,
though faded: white to grunge,

garish yellows, turquoise, neuralgic greens,
all weather-beaten pastels, colorless
as frocks laundered a hundred times
but good for another season—
and maybe one more...

Somewhere out there, decades ago,
Jane turned up on a Sunday morning,
nothing left of her
but red-haired bones with buckteeth
and both hands missing.

The road leans into the hill
we call White Wolf Grade:
an easy, unassuming acclivity
that tempts us to ignore the climb
from here on
and keep up to speed
as if still in the flatlands below,
lower and lower and farther off
as we ascend, elated,
inwardly lifted
because the ubiquitous haze
only locals know how to live with
has been washed away
(for now)—
the air absolved by
no more than a sprinkling,
an aspersion of rain.

Forty miles across the Valley floor
on the Elk Hills, we can see
smoke from the cogen plant
like the shroud
left behind by a ghost
who finally found the way out
of his bitterness:
one more malcontent
yearning for megalopolitan haunts.

But not this old man, oddly
gratified to be here—
hard scrabble San Joaquin fauna,
spawn of its austerity
and flourishing nowhere else:

Exultate Deo!

Even the wind, worn thin
by its long haul down from the North,
can linger here,
unwind in succulent grass,
relax and recoup before moving on.

Like us, it has survived, innocent
(or not) of all inclement weather
it's been blamed for.
And every secret overheard
rattling unlit windows
from town to town last night
has been forgotten,
has arrived here without baggage
and with nothing human to tell us.

Parked beside the road halfway up
to look and listen, we hear
only the wind *qua* wind:
breath, *numen,* inarticulate spirit.
And see...

Non-grata wildflower stragglers
disperse across the hillside
on their own trail of tears,
stumbling along like the Kawaiisu
to where the rez used to be
a few miles from here.

We've learned to make do,
we've had to,

with these smatterings that endure
in the drought years.

Exultate Deo!

Exactly: Insist on praise
despite lupines in rags, stunned,
barely rising above the grass
and tatterdemalion,
half-breed daisies of some sort.

That fortune in poppies we inherited
(remember them?)
has been squandered, leaving us
only a few ephemeral coins.

Goldenrods have gone bankrupt,
Chinese houses have died out,

and how long has it been
since pumas nibbled blue larkspur
like catnip, toxic or not;
since white wolves napped in the sun,
camouflaged by popcorn flowers?

We're left with residuum.
And yet, everything
nonbiblical we need to know
has been written here,
though more the scrawl of a dry pen
than calligraphy,
as if the fields were rough notes
for a finished manuscript
that's been lost.

No doubt the pages would disintegrate
if we touched them;
nevertheless:

Tolle. Lege.

Some new roads are palimpsests,
the old implicit beneath them;
but this one's uphill
from the abandoned route:
low-tech but sensitive to contours,
humble enough
to accept cattle tracks
that followed aboriginal paths.

Our road cuts straight through impediments.

And everyone knows what a fence means
(or used to). Even if
its posts are rotting in place,
slack barbed wire still insists
on its illusions:
Keep Out.

But we slip through
without wasting a thought on it,
unsnagged scofflaws,
and hobble down to less than half
of a single lane, one step across,
encroached on by creosote
that takes root in asphalt
and fractures it.

Though freeze and thaw pry open fissures,
scoop out potholes
the wind refills with sand,
this old road,
an indelible trace of the past,
will easily outlast us,
though less steadfast than Roman cobbles
or the mortars close by...

Kawaiisu bad luck to count them,
just asking for a rattlesnake bite,
but half-blind to time, we touch
pestled hollows scattered across bedrock

and pretend
to read them like Braille:

a legend of
ancient women gathered here to gab
and pound acorns into bitter flour
while their men hunted
jackrabbits with a sharp stick,
talking to the mountains.

This morning a splash of rainwater
darkens them all like wine,
but the lichen fused to granite
has already dried out,
coarse, bile yellow or black.
It must be as primordial
as the chalices themselves
that no one can lift
(*transeant a me calix iste*),
sunken into stone—forever stone
and never bread—
not even for unbelievers
to break their teeth on.

Why do we imagine
these mortars have worn deeper
since we came here years ago?
Impossible—unless
ghosts along with the weather
have been hard at work nonstop
on a new task:
grinding the time we've been given
into less than a handful
of grit.

And yet:
mounted in concrete
on the outcrop above us, persisting
on a local simulacrum of Golgotha,

no longer in use:
a white Easter sunrise service
cross.

Exultate Deo!

From here, we can see as far
as we look—at least
whenever the haze will let us.
An excellent site for megaliths,
for a Euro Stone Age ego trip,
but the Kawaiisu, slurred as Diggers,
inclined toward humility
and the nuanced musings of basketwork.

Our lowland grandfathers raised this cross,
stark and artless
rather than ornate Celtic,
welded from oil field steel: Executioners
would've had to rivet their victims to it.

Working stiffs in neckties, their wives
in millinery and white cotton gloves,
waited out in the chill for the sun
to come up over Bear Mountain;
mumbled unwieldy Victorian hymns
and worshiped, warming their hands
at pastoral canned heat,
half-listening,
and thought their own thoughts.

But they believed,

expecting their faith to be here for us
—and it is—
but never guessed that vandals
would dis the cross,
shinny up with black Krylon
to wildstyle its patibulum
with their own tags: indecipherable logos
instead of *REX IVDÆORUM*.

Rust is as close as we come
to cleansing blood,
beer bottles the only oblation.
Nevertheless, there's holiness here,
holy ground. A hush
surrounds the gossip stones
and, for a moment, every pestle
is laid aside
as quietness infuses us:

Christus resurrexit.

Risen indeed!

Corn Camp Road

You know what to expect from the sun,
already so vehement
early in the morning early in August
it can singe hair
on the cracked-leather back of your neck.

Otherwise, old man, your crepe skin
has been so thinned by meds
that a scratch bleeds like a gash.
Only literally thin-skinned, though,
you're neither on edge
nor easily offended anymore,
whose passions have turned to gristle;

whose thoughts have been fully rendered
this late in life,
left so long in so many summer fires
that only perseverance remains
to scrape burnt to a crust
from consciousness...

This month tests us all.

Nietzschean will shimmers in the heat,
insubstantial,
priests curse their collars,
and beer brawls break out in the park.
Every August staunch widows die
when their A/C goes down.
Sirens chafe us all night;
and at dawn, cops come home exhausted
to wives who want a divorce.

Therefore, hold on,
even though nothing you need
remains within reach.
Persist without an assigned task,
stubbornly insist,

wear down your weariness
and abide; wait it out;
stand firm: Endure:
Endure to the end:

hic salvus erit.

West on decrepit Main Street
past empty storefronts suffering
from dementia, glass
cataract-blurred by dirt
and fingerprints from decades ago;
ghost signs so faded on brick walls
no one can guess
what they keep trying to say.

On out of town and past
the postwar, classic California ranch houses
(low and wide with deep eaves
obfuscating shuttered windows)
built by arriviste Italian immigrant farmers
during cotton's long dominion;

houses where their wives survived
speaking no more English than the cats
and somehow wound down
at less than the speed of time, diehards
cloistered in their shadowy solariums.

And then west another mile or so
before turning onto Corn Camp Road
where one field has been abandoned,
overgrown with desiccated scrub—
unexpectedly handsome in gamboge,
burnt umber and khaki weeds,
or undecided between gray and brown
like mourning doves.

Even the leaves
of the lean mesquite, its branches
a snarl of galvanized wire,
are more gray than green.

But the next field, privileged
with costly, imported water,
flourishes, knee-deep in alfalfa
mowed and baled less than a month ago.
Hundreds of jittery moths
celebrate its eudaemonia
just across the ditch from desert.

And above both fields
—both alive—
you notice a thin cloud
of vultures: witnesses
rather than scavengers,
looking down on moths, on doves
with their Vox Humana,
on us, and on the blackbirds,
just as troubled as we are,
resisting grace,
packed into their own cumulonimbus.

Legends try to ignore time,
although nothing discourages it in the least,
laboring relentlessly
as if with case-hardened, glinting chisels
to chip more and more plaster
from these walls...

The Burnt School provides no dark niche
for ghosts to shelter in
all the interminable day:
The sun would salt them like slugs.

And even on moonlit nights,
when moths working the graveyard shift

glimmer above the fields
like ignes fatui,
these three walls cast no shadows
deep enough to hide them.

Therefore the ghosts haunt your mind,
now and then drifting out
into peripheral vision
where you can almost see them
unless you look.
But the dead are too quick.

And the actual fire?

Maybe a potbellied stove
seduced a curtain;
or it could have been ignited
by the custodian's foolish inner child
juggling hot coals;
by an unrepentant third grader
in the closet, obsessed
with protoerotic match flame;
by a Basque sheepherder,
whispering French smut
into the teacher's ear after school,
who flicked a butt in the wastebasket;
or by the wind, possibly,
complicit in so much malfeasance,
tipping over a candle
lit to commemorate Santa Lucia.

Silence accumulates in these ruins,
so intense it precludes
even written words,
keeping vandals at a distance,
intimidated: no graffiti.

But purple thistle, relentless,
scribbles along the margins of the road
an ill-tempered gloss,

its usual prickly disrespect
for anyone who passes by.

Spinas et tribulas germinabit tibi.

Roads around here stick to business,
strictly north-south, east-west,
as if laid out on the earth
with a straight edge—
no nuance, no nonsense
about following contours:

Our pioneers imposed their will,
convinced that civilization
exists only on a grid.

But this road, Main Drain, maunders—
an exception, intersecting
Corn Camp at an impromptu angle
and then looping back north,
aimless and serpentine,
acceding to the eccentricities
of an old canal
that traces its ancestry
back to an aboriginal slough.

This road stretches two easy crow miles
into ten, all curves.
Something about that offends us,
and a few stubborn drivers
have died here, refusing
to slow down
for mountain switchbacks
on such level land.

Turn west again at a country store,
ramshackle survivor of oil gluts
and plow-down crop prices,
its walls crusted with beer posters
like exanthemata.

Fieldhands and roustabouts still stop
for black sunrise coffee,
for an afternoon Bud.

But in less than a mile,
you shirk the quotidian,
turn south onto a dirt track,
and let dust cloud behind you
like angry wasps.

Buena Vista Slough drains the overflow
of one nonexistent lake
up the Valley to another—
beyond Lost Hills
where someone (but who?)
left Maria alone
and dead in its grubby thickets.

Here you see only desolation:
mummified willows that might
or might not come back to life
when rain finally breaks the curse;
tule reeds drier than raffia hair
on African devil masks.

Arid wetland, enduring
four dry seasons again this year,
hope withering in its roots,
nevertheless the slough knows how
to wait—
an almost lost art.

So you stop, willing to learn,
shut off the engine,
and listen to insects hum largo
the most placid tune you'll ever hear

while sunlight bears down,
determined to stifle them.

And not far off, running
parallel to this anachronism,
the deep, concrete California Aqueduct,
brimful of captive water,
flows the last hundred miles
south to Babylon...

All at once from the brush,
clattering in brittle grass
behind a gray, recumbent trunk,
an egret ascends—slowly,
as if weighed down
by our burdens,
glistering the pure whiteness
all other whites in this world
aspire to:
an ordinary bird transfigured,

vestimenta sunt alba sicut nix.

Holding your breath,
astonished and blessed
by its impossible, awkward grace,
you want to grab those dangled legs
and rise with it...

The track narrows from here on.
You straddle axle-cracking ruts
and hear branches screech: fingernails
reaching out to scratch paint
and lacerate nerves.

But slow down, be patient,
and their animus will become a harsh caress
that urges you on until
you jolt back to the asphalt again,
just beyond Corn Camp,
a few unhindered miles from home.

Quaking Aspen

for Chris

Smoke insinuates a lawless trash burn,
a mini-Gehenna; or it could be
grass smoldering somewhere in the hills,
a fire we keep an eye on
nervously. Some years
everything that can burn does.

So desolate here in autumn,
the seared leaves still green
but blotched with raw sienna:
summer, not dead yet, dying
of a slow, debilitating disease.

So dry even our hearts dehydrate,
making us uneasy
about where we've been,
about the long, withering seasons behind us
and how close winter is
no matter how stubbornly the heat persists.

But this old man has outlasted regret
and sluffed off despair, so far,
convinced that a few sips
of love
will sustain us
from here on, inexhaustible,
like the widow's scant flour and oil,
iuxta verbum Domini...

One Sunday late in October
more than thirty calendar years ago,
you and I climbed
out of our monochromatic valley
to visit a museum
of seasons,

a New England tableau
briefly on display high in the Sierras.

And we brought those colors home,
not the dried leaves
children would have gathered
and soon misplaced,
but an unfaded consciousness
kept vivid until now—
until this inevitable, inward autumn
we've come to,
still together, living
in our imagined landscape,
real only in the past, perhaps,
but nevertheless accessible
here on this googled earth:

Zoom in on the new road north,
an overlay on time, fervent
black asphalt with insistent stripes,
yellow that almost convinces us
it will never discolor.

That new highway has a textbook look—
taxes, engineers, and unlimited union labor:
Leviathan at work.
Not the road I remember,
narrow with crumbling shoulders—
infamous for head-ons,
for drunk drivers upended in a culvert—
washed out by flash floods every winter.

And some of its not-quite towns, bypassed
places with names
but no one to call them home,
long dead,
have been resurrected now.
Subdivided, they offer refuge—
a brutal, time-consuming commute,
but worth it:

Not a ghost town, but ghostly
in midmorning,
curtains on windows like shrouds
so old they'd disintegrate
if it ever occurred to anyone
to open them.

We drove to the end
of its only street and slowly back,
stopping at a clapboard store
to buy snacks. The clerk
said nothing, saw nothing in us—
like the dead looking into a mirror.

But beer stench from the saloon next door
reassured us: life—
nightlife at least,
or morose locals who drank all day,
keeping themselves in the dark.

In towns like that,
everyone wants out of the light.

The sun at noon could blister ectoplasm
and the moon set fire
to the tinder of a banshee's hair.

From one end of Main Street
to the other, you see no one,
and nothing moves except the dust
that goes round and round,
practicing the frantic dance
the devil taught it.

The packing shed had packed it in.
Decrepit, it sat like a huge skull
with its jaw wired
and sheets of warped plywood
nailed over its eyes,
not to keep sensory input out,
but to trap the past—

a bitter *ubi sunt*
only a few are alive to remember.

In '37 or so, when Mom
and her family drifted in from Route 66,
she went barefoot to the orange groves,
harvesting the gold
crated and shipped from that shed:
Sierra Sue, Spaniel, Terra Bella.

Oranges are still handpicked
and packed by hand,
some of the same brand names,
though everything is galvanized now,
rustproof—an illusion,
as if time couldn't chew through steel
as readily as wood.

The same scattering of battered cars
park on blacktop instead of dirt,
but no one is fooled
by the faux security
of chain link and guard shacks,
usually unmanned.

The old road east into the Sierras
had a shallow learning curve,
dawdled in tall grass below the foothills
among valley oaks, giants
either so ancient they'd be worshiped
in pagan Europe
or dead for years—snags
like weathered grave markers
above heaps of rotting branches:
excellent firewood, the best,
but forbidden now by eco-law.

And vanished from Google Earth,
the campground nearby
where I holed up one summer

in a lean year,
working too hard at a boneheaded job
and driving that deadly highway
home on weekends
to you and our toddler.

Farther up, the pond
that used to be a lake,
high on the dam and glittering:
Rings around the shore
keep a record
of its incremental descent
into emptiness. Drought
and bad luck, of course,
but also the whims
of government have sucked it dry.

Bluegills would take a close look at crickets,
and bass feeling their way
along the bottom
are willing enough to nibble
plastic worms in the murk,
but no one is fishing.

The boat ramp ends in weeds
more than a stone's throw
above the waterline.
And everywhere, trash bags
spill their guts like roadkill
not even the crows want to touch.

In the dead mountain town, disinterred
now by tourists and commuters,
the abandoned TB sanatorium
has come back to life as condos.

But some residents have heard
coughing in the dark,
though dry and bloodless,
and shivered in cold spots watching
despair condense in their clouded breath.

Others have endured sympathetic night sweats,
ached with phantom pain
from an excised rib,
or felt hopelessness take hold of them
on endless Sunday afternoons.

You and I saw the place boarded up
and the shrubs gone native,
the town itself ignored,
but undaunted;
and a few miles uphill we passed
the inevitable failed homestead:

The gate was chained
with three or four rusted padlocks,
the ruts overgrown that led
to the house and the barn behind it,
both half-finished for fifty years.
The windmill kept turning
above a dry well—
a bad habit never broken.

Who knows whose madness it was
to settle there
or which heir still paid the taxes,
suffering from his own delusions
and clinging to the deed
once held by a loner
who raised wilted, knee-high corn
to feed his gaunt cattle
and fed himself better
on bitterness.

Cor quod novit amaritudinum.

From here, for a few miles, the road
that used to follow the river,
when it could, still does,
accepting terrain too rugged
for engineers to finesse,

and then climbs—
an orange oscillation on the map,
jittery with switchbacks
that look just as wicked from orbit.

That other turbulent river
in which then becomes now
and now dissolves into then,
carries us along like two sticks,
not saturated, not yet,
nor snatched from the current.

But I suspect the whitewater
that elated us so much,
watching it churn over boulders
as if inexhaustible,
has been reduced to a trickle,
tempting vandals with Day-Glo Krylon
to gloss all that exposed surface—
which, according to their *Weltanschauung,*
would otherwise be wasted.

Close to the summit, unpaved side roads
crisscross through the woods
among vacation cabins
and the permanent getaways
of misfits with mountain blood,
thin skin, and simple needs,
mostly for a tavern with beer on tap
and some chairs to toss.

And here's that historic lodge
from which Bonnie checked out,
shot dead by a left-handed proxy
while she slept with her lover
from the rez
who survived his head wound.

All this less than five years
after our visit
on an unhaunted All Hallows' Eve
before fake blood good enough to fool anyone,
before the license to undress
and the mud lust we live with now.

Aspens wore their bonfire costumes,
a harmless masque rather than bacchanal,
and danced for us
in the muted, andante wind.

That afternoon on the far side of the summit,
we parked and walked for awhile
in lucid air, in exhilarating dazzle,
lumen de lumine—
not merely caught and reflected
but a source, as if every leaf
contained its own inner light.

Neither of us young nor naïve,
we took to love as if new to it
and held on—held
to the unlikely idea of *us,*
almost untenable in this world.

The pines hummed overhead,
incense cedar bowed a cello note,
and faithful dogwood stood by.
Our kisses went on and on
back then, *ad infinitum*
coming too quickly to an end.

We've lived ever since suspended
in that one autumn afternoon,
kept the turning leaves as they were—
gold, citron, copper, burnt orange,
an unchanging anamnesis, no matter
how many actual seasons
have had at us,
with freeze and thaw or relentless heat.

Some would imagine
that those aspens were waiting on the Lord,
the leaves alone together,
each trembling with its own anticipation.
And among them,
as far as earth can offer it,
we found peace that could,
potentially at least,
endure.
And it has.

A Note on the Latin

The Latin scattered through the text is neither macaronic nor pretentious. It's no surprise that I don't know the language; I studied it briefly once, but soon bogged down. But I do have some reasons for inserting the quotations in addition to the fun of it and the feeling that it adds an interesting element to the texture of the poems. In keeping with the overall motif of road trips, I could call them speed bumps intended to slow down the reader. I get going a little too fast through a longish poem, and I doubt that I'm unusual. Also, the Latin provides commentary rather than advancing the narrative—a sort of *Selah*: "Pause and think about it" is a common translation of the notation that appears so often in the Book of Psalms. Finally, Latin allows me to say things that might make some readers uneasy and perhaps keep them from reading something I hope they will enjoy. All biblical quotations are taken from the Vulgate.

"Granite Road":
panem nostrum... our daily bread
in loco fumus... (macaronic) in the place of smoke (from *in loco parentis*)
Dona nos pacem... Give us peace

"White Wolf Grade":
Exultate Deo... Rejoice in the Lord
Tolle. Lege... Take up and read (Augustine's *Confessions*)
REX... King of the Jews (Matthew 27:37)
Christus... Christ is Risen

"Corn Camp Road":
hic salvus... This one will be saved
Spinas et... Thorns and thistles it shall grow for you (Genesis 3:18)
vestimenta sunt... clothing as white as snow (Matthew 28:3)

"Quaking Aspen":
iuxta verbum... according to the word of the Lord
ubi sunt... Where are [they]? (consult any glossary of literary terms)
Cor quod... The heart knows its own bitterness (Proverbs 14:10)
lumen de lumine... light from light
ad infinitum... the familiar: again and again, forever

Acknowledgments

From Here On appeared originally in *Pilgrim: A Journal of Catholic Experience,* each section in a quarterly edition posted during 2016.

Cover artwork, "Bare Trees Against Sky During Sunset," unattributed; author photo by Chris Thompson; cover and interior book design by Diane Kistner; Hoefler text and titling

About FutureCycle Press

FutureCycle Press is dedicated to publishing lasting English-language poetry books, chapbooks, and anthologies in both print-on-demand and Kindle ebook formats. Founded in 2007 by longtime independent editor/publishers and partners Diane Kistner and Robert S. King, the press incorporated as a nonprofit in 2012. A number of our editors are distinguished poets and writers in their own right, and we have been actively involved in the small press movement going back to the early seventies.

The FutureCycle Poetry Book Prize and honorarium is awarded annually for the best full-length volume of poetry we publish in a calendar year. Introduced in 2013, our Good Works projects are anthologies devoted to issues of universal significance, with all proceeds donated to a related worthy cause. Our Selected Poems series highlights contemporary poets with a substantial body of work to their credit; with this series we strive to resurrect work that has had limited distribution and is now out of print.

We are dedicated to giving all of the authors we publish the care their work deserves, making our catalog of titles the most diverse and distinguished it can be, and paying forward any earnings to fund more great books.

We've learned a few things about independent publishing over the years. We've also evolved a unique, resilient publishing model that allows us to focus mainly on vetting and preserving for posterity poetry collections of exceptional quality without becoming overwhelmed with bookkeeping and mailing, fundraising activities, or taxing editorial and production "bubbles." To find out more, come see us at www.futurecycle.org.

www.ingramcontent.com/pod-product-compliance
Lightning Source LLC
Chambersburg PA
CBHW070452050426
42451CB00015B/3451